Listening and Speaking English Workbook

Book 1 - Beginners

ISBN-13: 9781772452792

Version 2.0 August 2018

About Complete Test Preparation Inc.

The Complete Test Preparation Team has been publishing high quality study materials since 2005. Over 1 million students visit our websites every year, and thousands of students, teachers and parents all over the world (over 100 countries) have purchased our teaching materials, curriculum, study guides and practice tests.

Complete Test Preparation is committed to providing students with the best study materials and practice tests available on the market. Members of our team combine years of teaching experience, with experienced writers and editors, all with advanced degrees.

Published by
Complete Test Preparation Inc.
Victoria BC Canada

Visit us on the web at https://www.efl-esl.com
Printed in the USA

FEEDBACK

We welcome your feedback. Email us at feedback@efl-esl.com with your comments and suggestions. We carefully review all suggestions and often incorporate reader suggestions into upcoming versions. As a Print on Demand Publisher, we update our products frequently.

Contents

Getting Started

Welcome! Each lesson section has a QR code to access audio files.

What is a QR Code? A QR code looks like a barcode and it's used as a shortcut to link to content online using your phone's camera, saving you from typing lengthy addresses into your mobile browser.

LESSON 1
DAISY AND GEORGE

VOCABULARY - LISTEN AND REPEAT

hello	yes	no	name	listen
a	woman	woman's	man	man's I
am	is	my	Canadian	her his

LISTEN:

Hello, my name is Daisy.
Hello, my name is George.

Daisy is a woman.
I am a woman.
George is a man.
I am a man.

LISTEN TO THE SENTENCES BELOW, COVER THE ANSWERS ON THE RIGHT, AND THEN ANSWER THE QUESTIONS

 QUESTIONS

 ANSWERS

Questions	Answers
Is her name Daisy?	Yes, her name is Daisy.
Is his name George?	Yes, his name is George.
Am I a woman?	Yes, I am a woman.
Am I a man?	Yes, I am a man.
Is Daisy a woman?	Yes, Daisy is a woman.
Is George a man?	Yes, George is a man.

LISTEN TO THE SENTENCES BELOW, COVER THE ANSWERS ON THE RIGHT, AND THEN ANSWER THE QUESTIONS

George is a man's name.
Daisy is a woman's name.

QUESTIONS	ANSWERS
Is George a man's name?	Yes
Is George a woman's name?	No
Is Daisy a woman's name?	Yes
Is Daisy a man's name?	No

LISTEN:

George is Canadian.
Daisy is Canadian.

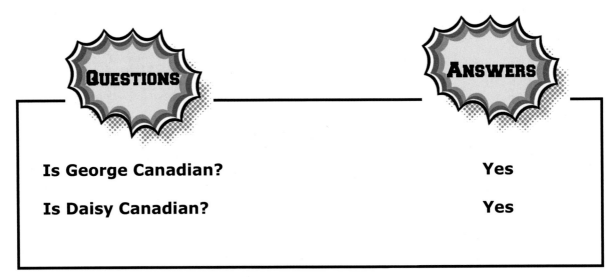

QUESTIONS	ANSWERS
Is George Canadian?	Yes
Is Daisy Canadian?	Yes

LESSON 2
TO BE OR NOT TO BE

VOCABULARY: LISTEN AND REPEAT

they	we	he	she	it
what	to be	verb	singular	one (1)
who	sentence	you	are	

LISTEN:

"To be" is a verb.
Singular is one (1).

To Be
Singular
I am
you are
he is
she is
it is

He is a man.
She is a woman.
It is a verb.

QUESTIONS	ANSWERS
Is he a man?	*Yes, he is a man.*
Is she a woman?	*Yes, she is a woman.*
Is "to be" a verb?	*Yes, "to be" is a verb.*

LISTEN

George is Canadian.

He is Canadian.

Daisy is Canadian.

She is Canadian.

COVER THE ANSWERS, THEN LISTEN TO THE QUESTIONS BELOW. ANSWER THE QUESTIONS IN SENTENCES.

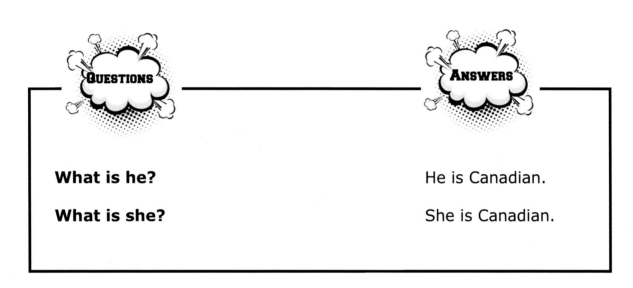

QUESTIONS	ANSWERS
What is he?	He is Canadian.
What is she?	She is Canadian.

12

COVER THE ANSWERS, THEN LISTEN TO THE QUESTIONS BELOW. ANSWER THE QUESTIONS IN SENTENCES.

QUESTIONS — **ANSWERS**

George is a man.

What is his name?　　　　　　His name is George.

Who is he?　　　　　　　　　He is George.

Daisy is a woman.

What is her name?　　　　　　Her name is Daisy.

Who is she?　　　　　　　　　*She is Daisy.*

LESSON 3 - HOW ARE YOU?

VOCABULARY: LISTEN AND REPEAT

how	fine	plural	teacher	teachers
your	friend	friends	Canadians	and

LISTEN

COVER THE ANSWERS, THEN LISTEN TO THE QUESTIONS BELOW. ANSWER THE QUESTIONS IN SENTENCES.

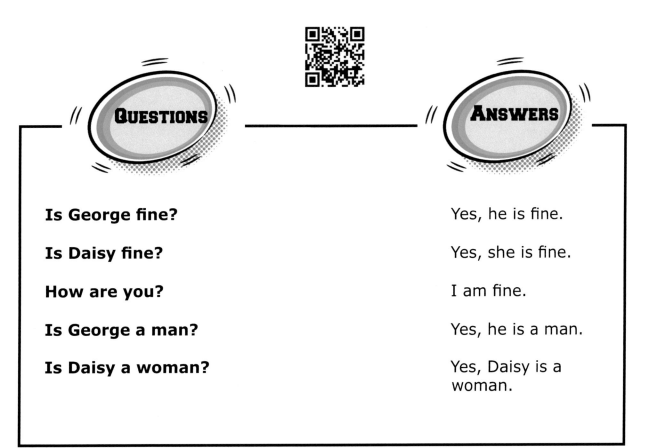

QUESTIONS	**ANSWERS**
Is George fine?	Yes, he is fine.
Is Daisy fine?	Yes, she is fine.
How are you?	I am fine.
Is George a man?	Yes, he is a man.
Is Daisy a woman?	Yes, Daisy is a woman.

LISTEN

**TO BE
Singular**

I am
you are
he is
she is
it is

I am Canadian.
You are Pakistani.
He is a man.
She is a woman.
It is a verb.

**TO BE
Plural**

we are
you are
they are

We are Canadians.
George and Daisy are teachers.
They are teachers.

COVER THE ANSWERS, THEN LISTEN TO THE QUESTIONS BELOW. ANSWER THE QUESTIONS IN SENTENCES.

QUESTIONS	ANSWERS
Are George and Daisy Canadians?	*Yes, they are Canadians.*
Are we teachers?	*Yes, you are teachers.*
How are you?	*I am fine*
How is your friend?	*My friend is fine.*
Are George and Daisy fine?	*Yes, they are fine.*
Are you and George and Daisy fine?	*Yes, we are fine.*
I am George.	
Who am I?	*You are George.*
I am Daisy.	
Who am I?	*You are Daisy.*

LESSON 4 - PETER'S DOG

VOCABULARY:

LISTEN AND REPEAT

| thank you | this | that | cell phone | dog |
| its | their | our | | |

LISTEN

This is Jane and Peter

Is that your dog?

Yes, it is my dog.

What is its name?

Its name is Toto.

COVER THE ANSWERS, THEN LISTEN TO THE QUESTIONS BELOW. ANSWER THE QUESTIONS IN SENTENCES.

 **QUESTIONS**

 **ANSWERS**

Questions	Answers
Is Peter a man?	*Yes, Peter is a man.*
How is Peter?	*He is fine.*
Is this his dog?	*Yes, it is his dog.*
What is its name?	*Its name is Toto.*

LISTEN

Singular

my
This is my cell phone.

your
That is your cell phone.

his
This is his dog.

her
This is Jane's cell phone. This is her cell phone.

its
Its name is Toto.

18

COVER THE ANSWERS, THEN LISTEN TO THE QUESTIONS BELOW. ANSWER THE QUESTIONS IN SENTENCES.

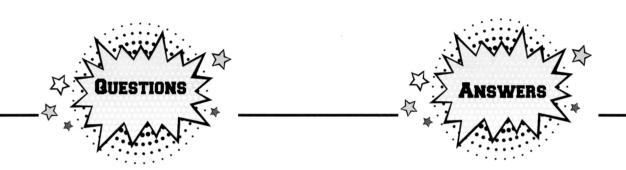

QUESTIONS	**ANSWERS**

What is Peter's dog's name?   *Its name is Toto.*

Is Toto Peter's dog?   *Yes, Toto is his dog.*

Are we your teachers?   *Yes, you are our teachers.*

Daisy has a cell phone.

Is it her cell phone?   *Yes, it is her cell phone.*

George and Daisy's dog is Fido.

What is their dog's name?   *Their dog's name is Fido.*

LESSON 5 - HOW MANY BIRDS?

VOCABULARY: LISTEN AND REPEAT

one	two	three	bird
birds	to hear	to count	how many

LISTEN

COVER THE ANSWERS, THEN LISTEN TO THE QUESTIONS BELOW. ANSWER THE QUESTIONS IN SENTENCES.

Questions	Answers
How is Daisy?	*She is fine.*
How is George?	*He is fine.*
How are they?	*They are fine.*

LISTEN

Count: one (1) two (2) three (3)

I hear one bird.

I hear two birds.

I hear three birds.

They are Canadian birds.

Continued

COVER THE ANSWERS, THEN LISTEN TO THE QUESTIONS BELOW. ANSWER THE QUESTIONS IN SENTENCES.

QUESTIONS

ANSWERS

Questions	Answers
You hear how many birds?	*I hear one bird.*
You hear how many birds	*I hear three birds.*
You hear how many birds?	*I hear two birds.*

LISTEN

This is our dog.

This is Peter and Jane's dog.

It is their dog.

Their friend is Nancy.

Nancy is Canadian.

Continued

22

COVER THE ANSWERS, THEN LISTEN TO THE QUESTIONS BELOW. ANSWER THE QUESTIONS IN SENTENCES.

QUESTIONS

ANSWERS

Questions	Answers
Is this a dog?	*Yes, it is a dog.*
Is this two birds?	*Yes, it is two birds.*
Is this a cell phone?	*Yes, it is a cell phone.*
This is Peter and Jane's dog.	
Is it their dog?	*Yes, it is their dog.*
Who is Peter and Jane's friend?	*Their friend is Nancy.*
Is she their friend?	*Yes, she is their friend.*
Is Nancy Canadian?	*Yes, she is Canadian.*

LESSON 6 - GABRIELLE AND BEN

VOCABULARY: LISTEN AND REPEAT

I'm	good-bye	to do	to say	to have
to ring	the	has		

Hello, Gabrielle.
This is Ben.
How are you?

Hello

I'm great!
How are you
Ben?

I'm fine.
I have a cell
phone.

I have a cell
phone, too.
Good-bye Ben.

Good-bye
Gabrielle.

COVER THE ANSWERS, THEN LISTEN TO THE QUESTIONS BELOW. ANSWER THE QUESTIONS IN SENTENCES.

QUESTIONS

ANSWERS

Who phones Gabrielle?	Ben phones Gabrielle.
How is Gabrielle?	She is great!
How is Ben?	He is fine.
Does Ben have a cell phone?	Yes, he has a cell phone.
Does Gabrielle have a cell phone?	Yes, she has a cell phone.
Do they say good-bye?	Yes, they say good-bye.

LISTEN

Count the cell phone rings:

one   two   three   four   five

LISTEN TO THE SENTENCES BELOW, COVER THE ANSWERS, AND THEN ANSWER THE QUESTIONS IN SENTENCES.

QUESTIONS	ANSWERS
How many rings do you hear?	I hear three rings.
How many rings do you hear?	I hear five rings.
How many rings do you hear?	I hear one ring
How many rings do you hear?	I hear two rings.
How many rings do you hear?	I hear four rings.

26

LISTEN

Plural

our

They are our dogs.

your

This is your dog.

their

They are Ben and Gabrielle's birds.
They are their birds.

LISTEN TO THE SENTENCES BELOW, COVER THE ANSWERS, AND THEN ANSWER THE QUESTIONS IN SENTENCES.

QUESTIONS	ANSWERS
Do Ben and Gabrielle have two birds?	*Yes, they have two birds.*
Do you hear four rings?	*Yes, I hear four rings.*

27

LESSON 7 - REVIEW

LISTEN TO THE SENTENCES BELOW, COVER THE ANSWERS, AND THEN ANSWER THE QUESTIONS IN SENTENCES.

ANSWER IN A SENTENCE

Answers

LISTEN
My name is George.

Am I a man?   Yes, I am a man.

Answers

LISTEN
My name is Daisy.
Am I a woman?   Yes, I am a woman.

Hello George, how are you?

I'm just great!

I'm fine, thank you.

How are you Daisy?

Do you hear the birds?

Are they your birds?

Yes, I hear the birds.

Yes, they are my birds.

Good bye

Good bye George

LISTEN TO THE SENTENCES BELOW, COVER THE ANSWERS, AND THEN ANSWER THE QUESTIONS IN SENTENCES.

QUESTIONS

ANSWERS

How is George?	*He is fine.*
How is Daisy?	*She is just great!*
Does George hear the birds?	*Yes, he hears the birds.*
Are they Daisy's birds?	*Yes, they are Daisy's birds.*
Do George and Daisy say "good bye?"	*Yes, they say "good bye."*

LISTEN

Gabrielle and Ben have cell phones.
Their friends have cell phones.
Ben likes to phone his friends.
Gabrielle likes to phone her friends.

LISTEN TO THE SENTENCES BELOW, COVER THE ANSWERS AND THEN ANSWER THE QUESTIONS IN SENTENCES.

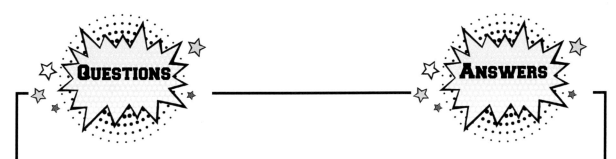

QUESTIONS	ANSWERS
Does Gabrielle have a cell phone?	*Yes, she has a cell phone.*
Does Ben have a cell phone?	*Yes, he has a cell phone.*
Who do they like to phone?	*They like to phone their friends.*
How many rings do you hear	*I hear two rings.*
How many rings do you hear?	*I hear four rings.*

TEST 1 - LESSONS 1 TO 7

Listen and type the number of the correct answer.
There are 10 questions. (1 mark each)
You are doing well if your mark is 8 or higher.

1. Is George Canadian?

  1 She is Canadian.
  2 She is Fine.
  3 Yes

2. Is George a man?

  1 George is a bird.
  2 George is Canadian.
  3 Yes, George is a man.

3. Is Daisy a woman's name?

  1 Yes, Daisy is a woman's name.
  2 It is a man's name.
  3 No.

4. George is Canadian. Is he Canadian?

  1 He is a man.
  2 Yes, he is Canadian.
  3 Yes, she is Canadian.

5. Daisy is fine. How is she?

  1 She is a woman.
  2 She is a man.
  3 She is fine.

6. George and Daisy are teachers. What are they?

1 They are dogs.
2 They are teachers.
3 They are Pakistanis.

7. What do you hear?

1 I hear a dog.
2 I hear Daisy.
3 I hear my friend.

8. Ben has a cell phone. What does he have?

1 He has a dog.
2 He has a bird.
3 He has a cell phone.

9. How many birds do you hear?

1 I hear one bird.
2 I hear three birds.
3 I hear four birds.

10. This is George's dog.

1 It is your dog.
2 It is his dog.
3 It is her dog.

ANSWERS

1. 3
Yes, George is Canadian.

2. 3
Yes, George is man.

3. 1
Yes, Daisy is a woman's name.

4. 2
They are teachers.

5. 3
She is fine.

6. 2
They are teachers.

7. 1
I hear a dog.

8. 3
He has a cell phone.

9. 2
I hear 3 birds.

10. 2
It is his dog

LESSON 8 - THE NEW CAR

VOCABULARY: **Listen and Repeat**

new	car	red	color	to phone
six	seven	notes		

LISTEN
Stephen phones George

YOU TALK FOR GEORGE AND LISTEN TO SEE IF YOU ARE CORRECT.

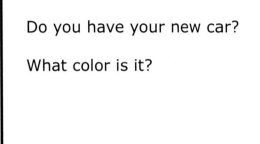

You

Hello, this is Stephen.

Do you have your new car?

What color is it?

You: *Hello*

You: *Hello, Stephen.*

You: *Yes, I have my new car.*

You: *It is red.*

LISTEN AND COUNT

Numbers: one, two, three, four, five, six, seven

LISTEN TO THE SENTENCES BELOW, COVER THE ANSWERS AND THEN ANSWER THE QUESTIONS IN SENTENCES.

 QUESTIONS

 ANSWERS

1. How many notes do you hear?   *I hear four notes.*

2. How many notes do you hear?   *I hear seven notes.*

3. How many notes do you hear?   *I hear six notes.*

1234567

LESSON 9 - SARAH PHONES CAROL

VOCABULARY: LISTEN AND REPEAT

dress   blue   thanks

Listen to Sarah and Carol

You Talk for Carol and Listen to See if You are Correct.

You: *Hello*

Hello, this is Sarah

You: *Hello, Sarah, how are you?*

I'm fine, thank you.

You: *I have a new dress.*

What color is it?

You: *It is blue.*

LISTEN TO THE SENTENCES BELOW, COVER THE ANSWERS AND THEN ANSWER THE QUESTIONS IN SENTENCES.

Questions

Answers

1. Who phones Carol?

Sarah phones Carol.

2. How is Sarah?

She is fine.

3. What does Carol have?

She has a new dress.

4. Who has a new dress?

Carol has a new dress.

5. What color is her dress?

It is blue.

6. Is Sarah a woman's name?

Yes, it is a woman's name.

7. How many notes do you hear?

I hear seven notes.

LESSON 10 - FRIENDLY TEACHERS

VOCABULARY: LISTEN AND REPEAT

| English | today | friendly | student | eight |
| nine | ten | dresses | women | an |

Hello English student. How are you today?

I am fine, thanks.

We are your friendly teachers. You are our friendly students.

Yes, we are.

Are you our friendly students?

LISTEN TO THE SENTENCES BELOW, COVER THE ANSWERS AND THEN ANSWER THE QUESTIONS IN SENTENCES.

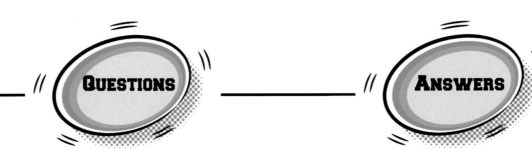

QUESTIONS	ANSWERS
1. Are we friendly teachers?	**Yes, you are friendly teachers.**
2. Are you a friendly student?	**Yes, I am a friendly student.**
3. How are you today?	**I am fine, thanks.**

012345678910

LISTEN TO THE SENTENCES BELOW, COVER THE ANSWERS AND THEN ANSWER THE QUESTIONS IN SENTENCES.

QUESTIONS	ANSWERS
How many new dresses does Carol have?	*She has one new dress.*
Is Carol a woman's name?	*Yes, Carol is a woman's name.*
Does Carol have a dress?	*Yes, Carol has a dress.*
Do women have dresses?	*Yes, they have dresses.*
Do you have friends?	*Yes, I have friends.*
Is Stephen a man's name?	*Yes, Stephen is a man's name.*

LESSON 11 - GEORGE'S NEW CAR

VOCABULARY:

whose   to talk

LISTEN AND REPEAT

some   for   cool

LISTEN

George has a new red car.

You have a cell phone.

George and Daisy have some birds.

Carol has a new dress.

We talk to our friends.

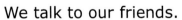

LISTEN TO THE SENTENCES BELOW, COVER THE ANSWERS AND THEN ANSWER THE QUESTIONS IN SENTENCES USING: MY, YOUR, HIS, HER, IT, OUR, THEIR

George has a new red car.
Whose car is it?

It is his car.

You have a cell phone.
Whose cell phone is it?

It is my cell phone.

George and Daisy have some birds.
Whose birds are they?

They are their birds.

Carol has a new dress.
Whose dress is it?

It is her dress.

We talk to some friends.
Who do we talk to?

We talk to our friends.

CAROL

You: *Hello*

Hello George. This is Carol.

You: *How are you?*

I'm fine. Do you have your new car?

You: *Yes, I have my car*

Is it new?

You: *Yes, it is new.*

Is it red?

You: *Yes, it is red.*

That is cool!
Good bye George.

You: *Good bye Carol.*

LISTEN AND COUNT

How many notes do you hear?   *I hear six notes.*

How many notes do you hear?   *I hear ten notes.*

How many notes do you hear?   *I hear eight notes.*

LESSON 12 - TOMS MOTORCYCLE

VOCABULARY: LISTEN AND REPEAT

motorcycle   silver   to like   to drive   town
too

LISTEN

Tom has a new motorcycle. It is red and silver.
He likes to drive to town. His friend Peter has a motorcycle, too.
They like to drive to town.

LISTEN TO THE SENTENCES BELOW, COVER THE ANSWERS AND THEN ANSWER THE QUESTIONS IN SENTENCES

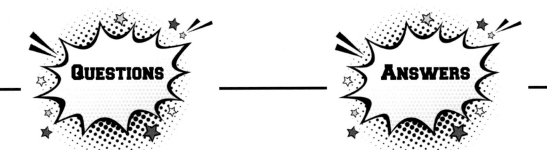

QUESTIONS	ANSWERS
Who has a new motorcycle?	**Tom has a new motorcycle.**
What does he like to do?	**He likes to drive to town.**
Does Peter have a motorcycle?	**Yes, he has a motorcycle.**
What color is Tom's motorcycle?	**It is red and silver**
What do Peter and Tom like to do?	**They like to drive to town.**

51

CAROL PHONES TOM - NOW YOU TALK FOR TOM

TOM (YOU)

You: Hello

Hello Tom, this is Carol.
How are you?

You: I'm fine, thanks.

Do you have a new
motorcycle?

You: Yes, I have a new motorcycle

What color is it?

It is red and silver.

That is cool!
Good-bye Tom.

Good-bye Carol

LESSON 13 - FRIENDS AT THE RESTURANT

VOCABULARY: LISTEN AND REPEAT

in   restaurant   orange   music   to order

Listen
You have two friends.
You are in a restaurant.
You hear music.
Your friends order orange juice.
You order orange juice, too.

LISTEN TO THE SENTENCES BELOW, COVER THE ANSWERS AND THEN ANSWER THE QUESTIONS IN SENTENCES

 QUESTIONS

 ANSWERS

Questions	Answers
How many friends do you have?	I have two friends.
Are you in a restaurant?	Yes, I am in a restaurant.
What do you hear?	I hear music.
Do you like the music? (yes)	Yes, I like the music.
What do your friends order?	They order orange juice.
What do you order?	I order orange juice.

54

You and your friends like to talk.

You: Yes, I like the music.

You: I like this restaurant.

ANSWER YOUR FRIENDS

You

Friend 1: I like the music. Do you like the music?

You: *Yes, I like the music.*

Friend 2: I like this juice. What do you like?

You: *I like this restaurant.*

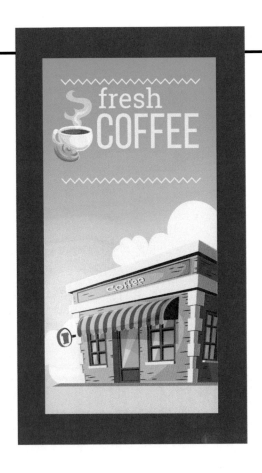

LISTEN TO THE SENTENCES BELOW, COVER THE ANSWERS AND THEN ANSWER THE QUESTIONS IN SENTENCES

How many friends are in the restaurant?

Two friends are in the restaurant

What do you hear?

I hear music.

What do you order?

I order orange juice.

What do your friends like to do in the restaurant?

They like to talk.

LESSON 14 - REVIEW

Your friend is a man. You phone him on your cell phone. Cover the right column and talk with your friend!

YOUR FRIEND	YOU
	Hello
Hello, how are you today?	
	I'm fine thanks.
Do you have your new car?	
	Yes, I have my new car.
What color is it?	
	It is silver and blue.
That is cool! Good bye.	
	Good bye.

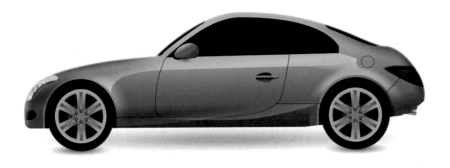

Your friend is a woman. You phone her on your cell phone. Cover the right column and talk with your friend!

YOUR FRIEND	**YOU**
	Hello
Hello, how are you today?	
	I'm fine thanks.
Do you have your new car?	
	Yes, I have my new car.
What color is it?	
	It is silver and blue.
That is cool! Good bye.	
	Good bye.

LISTEN TO THE SENTENCES BELOW, COVER THE ANSWERS AND THEN ANSWER THE QUESTIONS IN SENTENCES

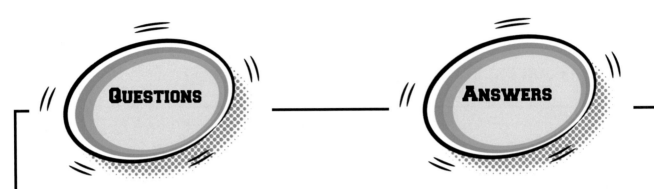

QUESTIONS	ANSWERS

Do you like music?   (yes)

Yes, I like music.

Do your friends like orange juice? (yes)

Yes, my friends like

orange juice.

How many notes do you hear?

I hear ten notes.

Are you an English student?
student.

Yes, I am an English

Is Sarah a girl's name?
name.

Yes, Sarah is a girl's

Tom has a new motorcycle.
Whose motorcycle is it?

It is Tom's motorcycle.

Are we your teachers?

Yes, you are our teachers.

Does your phone ring?

Yes, my phone rings.

TEST 2 - LESSONS 8 TO 14

Listen and type the number of the correct answer.
There are 10 questions. (1 mark each)
You are doing well if your mark is 8 or higher.

1.   Your friend has a new car.
  What does your friend have?

  1)   My friend has a motorcycle.
  2)   My friend has a new car.
  3)   My friend has some juice.

2.   How many notes do you hear?

  1)   I hear 10 notes
  2)   I hear 2 notes.
  3)   I hear 7 notes.

3. Sarah has a new dress.
What does Sarah have?

  1)   She has a new dress.
  2)   She has a new car.
  3)   She has a bird.

4. Are we your teachers?

  1)   We are students.
  2)   We are friends.
  3)   We are your teachers.

5. George and Daisy have some birds.
What do they have?

  1)   They have some juice.
  2)   They have some birds.
  3)   They have some cell phones.

6. How are you?

   1)   I am eight.
   2)   I am cool.
   3)   I am fine, thanks.

**7. Tom's motorcycle is red and silver.
What color is it?**

   1)   It is red.
   2)   It is red and silver.
   3)   It is blue.

8. What do you hear?

   1)   I hear music.
   2)   I hear a car.
   3)   I hear my friends.

**9. You order orange juice in a restaurant.
What do you order?**

   1)   I order music.
   2)   I order orange juice.
   3)   I order a car.

**10. Tom drives his motorcycle to town.
What does Tom drive?**

   1)   He drives his car.
   2)   He drives to town.
   3)   He drives his motorcycle.

ANSWERS

1. 2
My friend has a new car.

2. 3
I hear 7 notes.

3. 1
She has a new dress.

4. 3
We are your teachers.

5. 2
They have some birds.

6. 3
I am fine, thanks.

7. 2
It is red and silver.

8. 1
I hear music.

9. 2
I order orange juice.

10. 3
He drives his motorcycle.

Made in the USA
Las Vegas, NV
30 September 2023